GRAPHIC SCIENCE

UNDERSTANDING

VIRUSES

WITH MAX AXIOM

SUPER SCIENTIST

by Agnieszka Biskup

illustrated by Nick Derington

Consultant:

Wade A. Bresnahan, PhD

Associate Professor

Department of Microbiology

University of Minnesota

Capstone press

Mankato, Minnesota

Graphic Library is published by Capstone Press,
151 Good Counsel Drive, P.O. Box 669, Mankato, Minnesota 56002.
www.capstonepress.com

1 2 3 4 5 6 14 13 12 11 10 09

Library of Congress Cataloging-in-Publication Data
Biskup, Agnieszka.
Understanding viruses with Max Axiom, super scientist / by Agnieszka Biskup;
illustrated by Nick Derington.
p. cm. — (Graphic library. Graphic science)
Includes bibliographical references and index.
Summary: "In graphic novel format, follows the adventures of Max Axiom as he
explains the science behind viruses" — Provided by publisher.
ISBN-13: 978-1-4296-2338-4 (hardcover)
ISBN-10: 1-4296-2338-1 (hardcover)
ISBN-13: 978-1-4296-3453-3 (softcover pbk.)
ISBN-10: 1-4296-3453-7 (softcover pbk.)
1. Viruses — Juvenile literature. 2. Virus diseases — Juvenile literature. I. Derington,
Nick, ill. II. Title.
QR365.B57 2009
579.2 — dc22   2008029654

Set Designer
Bob Lentz

Book Designer
Alison Thiele

Cover Artist
Tod G. Smith

Editor
Christopher L. Harbo

Photo illustration credits: iStockphoto/Tony Sanchez, 13

TABLE of CONTENTS

CELLS

Cells are the basic structural unit of all living things. People are made up of trillions of cells. We have about 200 different kinds of specialized cells, including bone cells, skin cells, and blood cells.

Viruses are much smaller than bacteria. They're so small that you can't see them with a regular microscope.

You need a powerful electron microscope like this one to see them.

ELECTRON MICROSCOPE

A regular microscope uses light to magnify objects up to about 2,000 times.

But electron microscopes use tiny particles called electrons to magnify objects a million times and more.

Here's a virus that causes the common cold.

In order to reproduce, a virus first finds a living cell called a host.

Viruses can attack plant cells, animal cells, or bacteria.

VIRUS

HOST CELL

Most viruses reproduce in specific cells of certain organisms.

For example, the virus that causes the common cold reproduces in the cells of the nose and throat.

The virus enters the cell or injects its genetic material inside the host.

DORMANT VIRUSES

Some viruses can live in cells without harming them. They insert their genetic material, but no viruses are made immediately. They can stay inactive in the cell for long periods of time, until some change or stress activates them.

Once the genetic material is inside, it takes over the host. It turns the cell into a factory for viruses.

The viruses break out of the host cell, bursting and killing it.

But some viruses use a different method to escape. They push through the cell in a process called budding.

Budding may weaken a host cell, but it doesn't kill it immediately.

Either way, the new viruses are ready to find more cells to infect. Then they make more viruses.

Viruses can multiply very quickly. As more cells are damaged or killed, sickness or disease may result.

17

21

Schools and churches were closed.

Quarantines were set up to keep people from gathering together.

The 1918 flu killed tens of millions of people worldwide.

The flu can be controlled by vaccinating people. Vaccines are made with flu varieties most likely to spread and infect people.

But even with flu shots, people may still get sick. Doctors may choose the wrong varieties or the flu virus could change.

MORE ABOUT VIRUSES

We usually only hear about bad bacteria and ways to get rid of them. But only a small percentage of bacteria is truly harmful. In fact, many bacteria are very helpful. Without bacteria, we couldn't turn milk into cheese, sour cream, or yogurt. We use bacteria to help produce antibiotics and other medicines. Bacteria are even used to clean up oil spills.

Viruses can cause the colorful streaks and patterns you see in the petals of some tulips.

Having a fever is not always bad. Many viruses and bacteria don't grow as well when your body temperature rises above normal. A fever is often just your body trying to defend itself against infection.

Animals get sick from viruses too. That's why it's important to get your pets vaccinated against rabies, distemper, and other diseases.

Genetic mutations can sometimes allow a virus to jump from animals to humans. For example, pigs and birds can get the flu. In some cases, they can pass it on to people.

The virus known as HIV causes the serious disease called AIDS. HIV attacks the immune system, reducing its ability to fight off disease. HIV is spread only through direct contact with an infected person's bodily fluids, such as blood. Right now, there is no cure or vaccine for HIV infection or AIDS. Some medications, however, can help people with HIV live longer lives.

Vaccines aren't just for viruses. They're also used to protect people against some diseases caused by bacteria. Scientists have made vaccines for bacteria such as diphtheria, pertussis (whooping cough), and tetanus.

 A computer virus is a computer program that copies itself. It is passed between computers like a virus is passed from person to person. And just like a regular virus, computer viruses can be harmful. They can delete data and steal personal information.

MORE ABOUT

SUPER SCIENTIST

Real name: Maxwell J. Axiom
Hometown: Seattle, Washington
Height: 6' 1"   Weight: 192 lbs
Eyes: Brown   Hair: None

Super capabilities: Super intelligence; able to shrink to the size of an atom; sunglasses give x-ray vision; lab coat allows for travel through time and space.

Origin: Since birth, Max Axiom seemed destined for greatness. His mother, a marine biologist, taught her son about the mysteries of the sea. His father, a nuclear physicist and volunteer park ranger, schooled Max on the wonders of earth and sky.

One day on a wilderness hike, a megacharged lightning bolt struck Max with blinding fury. When he awoke, Max discovered a newfound energy and set out to learn as much about science as possible. He traveled the globe earning degrees in every aspect of the field. Upon his return, he was ready to share his knowledge and new identity with the world. He had become Max Axiom, Super Scientist.

GLOSSARY

bacteria (bak-TIR-ee-uh) — one-celled, tiny organisms that can be found throughout nature; many bacteria are useful, but some cause disease.

DNA (dee-en-AY) — the molecule that carries all of the instructions to make a living thing and keep it working

HIV (AYCH-ie-vee) — the virus that causes AIDS; HIV attacks the body's immune system, making patients more likely to get other illnesses.

immune system (i-MYOON SISS-tuhm) — the part of the body that protects against germs and diseases

influenza (in-floo-EN-zuh) — an illness that is like a bad cold with fever and muscle pain; a virus causes influenza.

mutation (myoo-TAY-shuhn) — a permanent change in nature, form, or quality; when viruses mutate they sometimes become stronger and more dangerous.

pathogen (PATH-uh-juhn) — a germ that causes diseases

polio (POH-lee-oh)— an infectious viral disease that attacks the brain and spinal cord

quarantine (KWOR-uhn-teen) — limiting or forbidding the movement of people to prevent the spread of disease

RNA (AHR-en-ay) — a molecule found in all cells that carries instructions for making proteins

vaccine (vak-SEEN) — a substance used to protect people and animals against disease

READ MORE

Herbst, Judith. *Germ Theory*. Great Ideas of Science. Minneapolis: Twenty-First Century Books, 2008.

Kite, Patricia L. *Unicellular Organisms*. Sci-Hi Life Science. Chicago: Raintree, 2008.

Krohn, Katherine. *The 1918 Flu Pandemic*. Disasters in History. Mankato, Minn.: Capstone Press, 2008.

Nye, Bill. *Bill Nye the Science Guy's Great Big Book of Tiny Germs*. New York: Hyperion, 2005.

Snedden, Robert. *A World of Microorganisims*. Microlife. Chicago: Heinemann, 2007.

INTERNET SITES

FactHound offers a safe, fun way to find educator-approved Internet sites related to this book.

Here's what you do:

1. Visit *www.facthound.com*
2. Choose your grade level.
3. Begin your search.

This book's ID number is 9781429623384.

FactHound will fetch the best sites for you!

INDEX